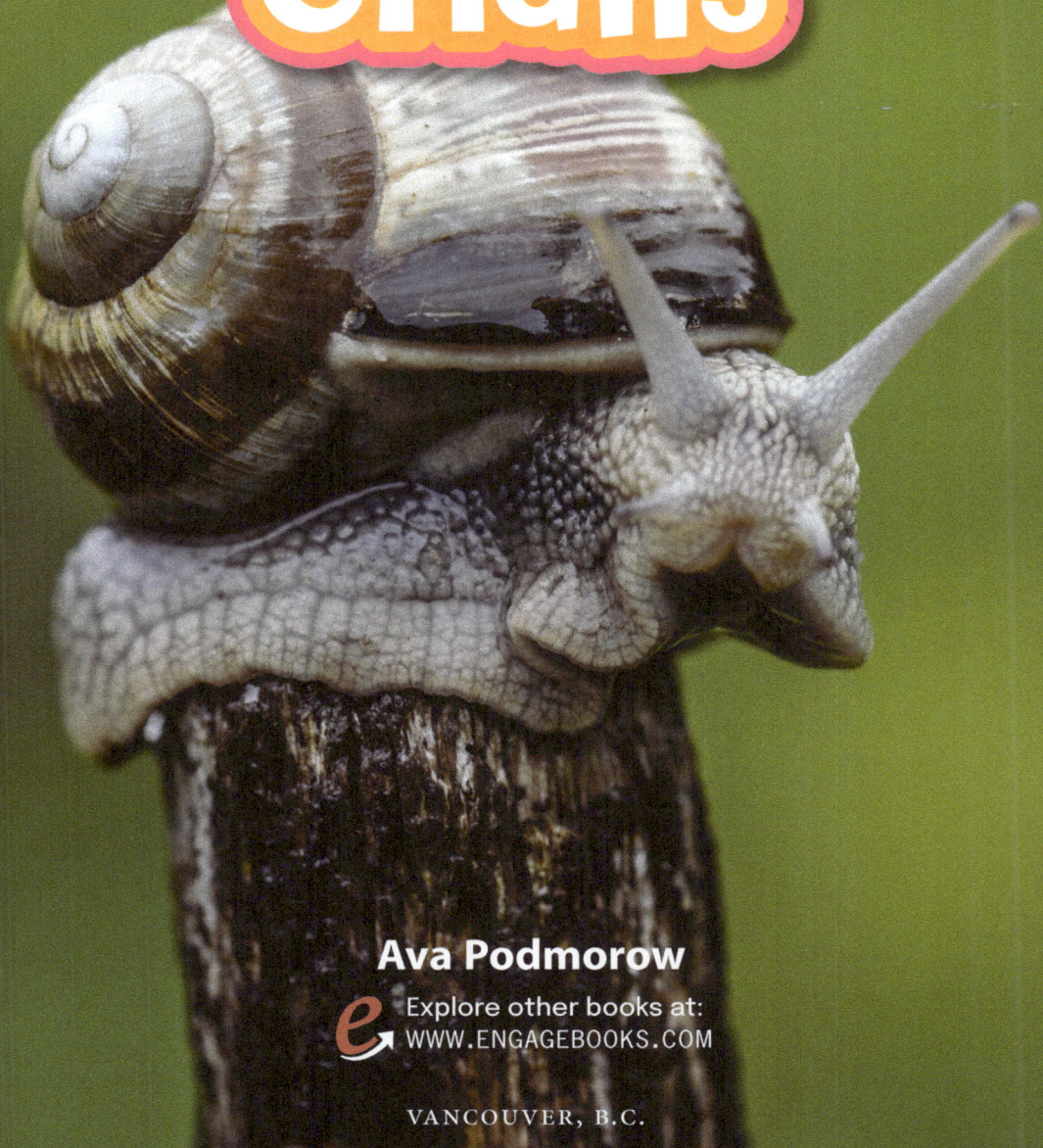

Backyard
Bugs
& Creepy-
Crawlies

Snails

Ava Podmorow

Explore other books at:
WWW.ENGAGEBOOKS.COM

VANCOUVER, B.C.

www.engagebooks.com

Snails: Level Pre-1
Backyard Bugs & Creepy Crawlies
Podmorow, Av 2004 –
Text © 2022 Engage Books
Design © 2022 Engage Books

Edited by: A.R. Roumanis
and Sarah Harvey

Text set in Epilogue

FIRST EDITION / FIRST PRINTING

LIBRARY AND ARCHIVES CANADA CATALOGUING IN PUBLICATION

Title: Snails / Ava Podmorow.
Names: Podmorow, Ava, author.
Description: Series statement: Backyard bugs & creepy-crawlies
Engaging readers: level pre-1, beginner.

Identifiers: Canadiana (print) 20220403511 | Canadiana (ebook) 2022040352X
ISBN 978-177476-724-5 (hardcover)
ISBN 978-177476-725-2 (softcover)
ISBN 978-177476-726-9 (epub)
ISBN 978-177476-727-6 (pdf)

Subjects:
LCSH: Snails—Juvenile literature.

Classification: LCC QL430.4 .P63 2022 | DDC J594/.3—DC23

This project has been made possible in part by the Government of Canada.

Canada

Snails live life in slow motion!

Snails live where it is wet.

They like forests and rain.

Snails need
to stay wet
and cool.

They hide
from the Sun
under plants.

Snail shells can be brown, yellow or pink.

Snail shells protect their soft bodies.

Shells grow larger as snails get older.

Snails can stay awake for thirty hours at a time!

They sleep inside their shells.

Some snails are as small as a pea.

Others are as long
as a dinner fork!

Snails have over one thousand tiny teeth.

Snails will eat just about anything.

Some snails even eat moss at the tops of trees!

Snails do not
see very well.

Their tentacles let
them know when
things move.

Tentacles

Snails can not see any colors.

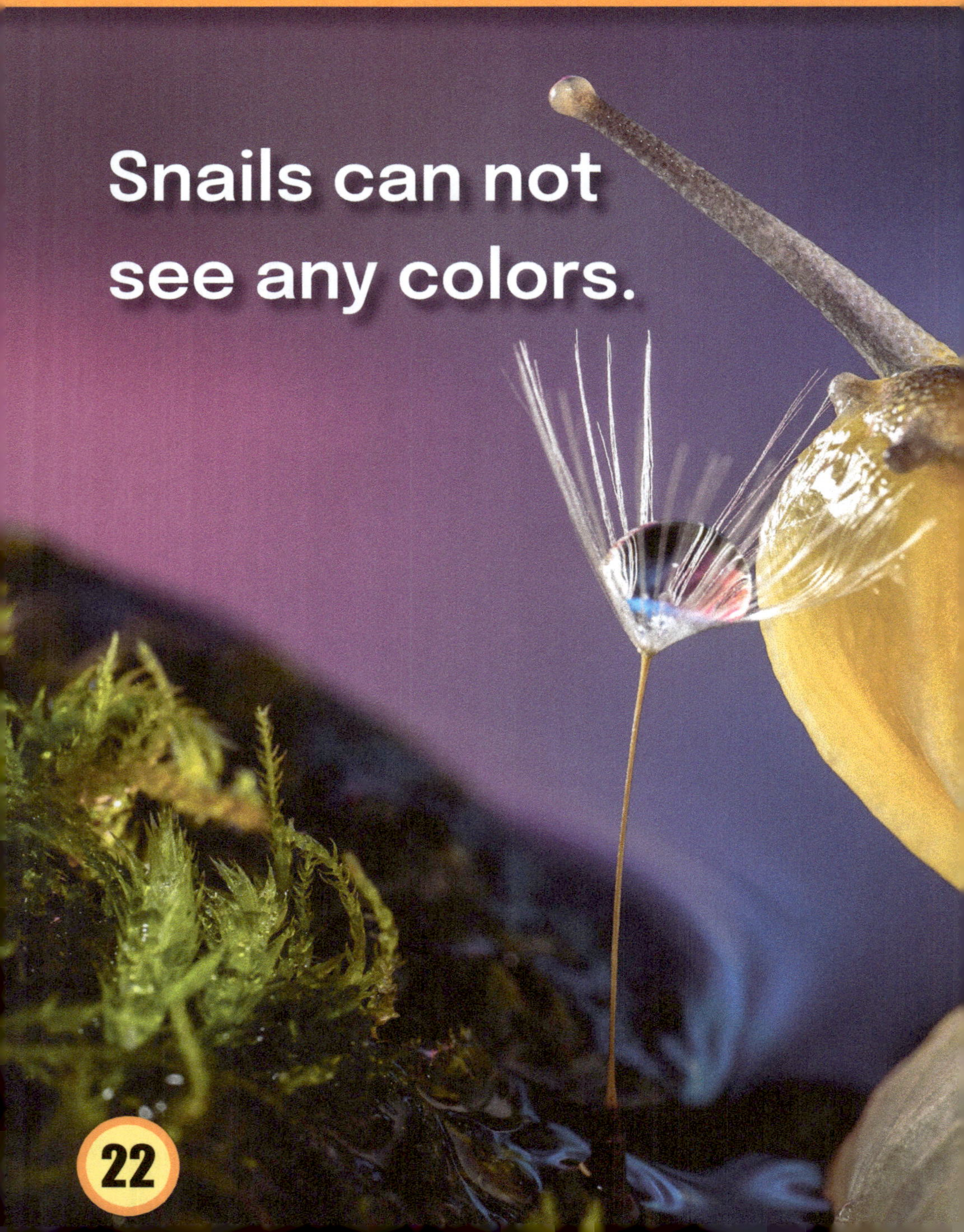

They are only able
to tell when it is
dark or light out.

Most snails live for about five years.

Some snails live
for fifteen years.

Snails move very slowly.

They can only move the length of a baseball bat in one hour!

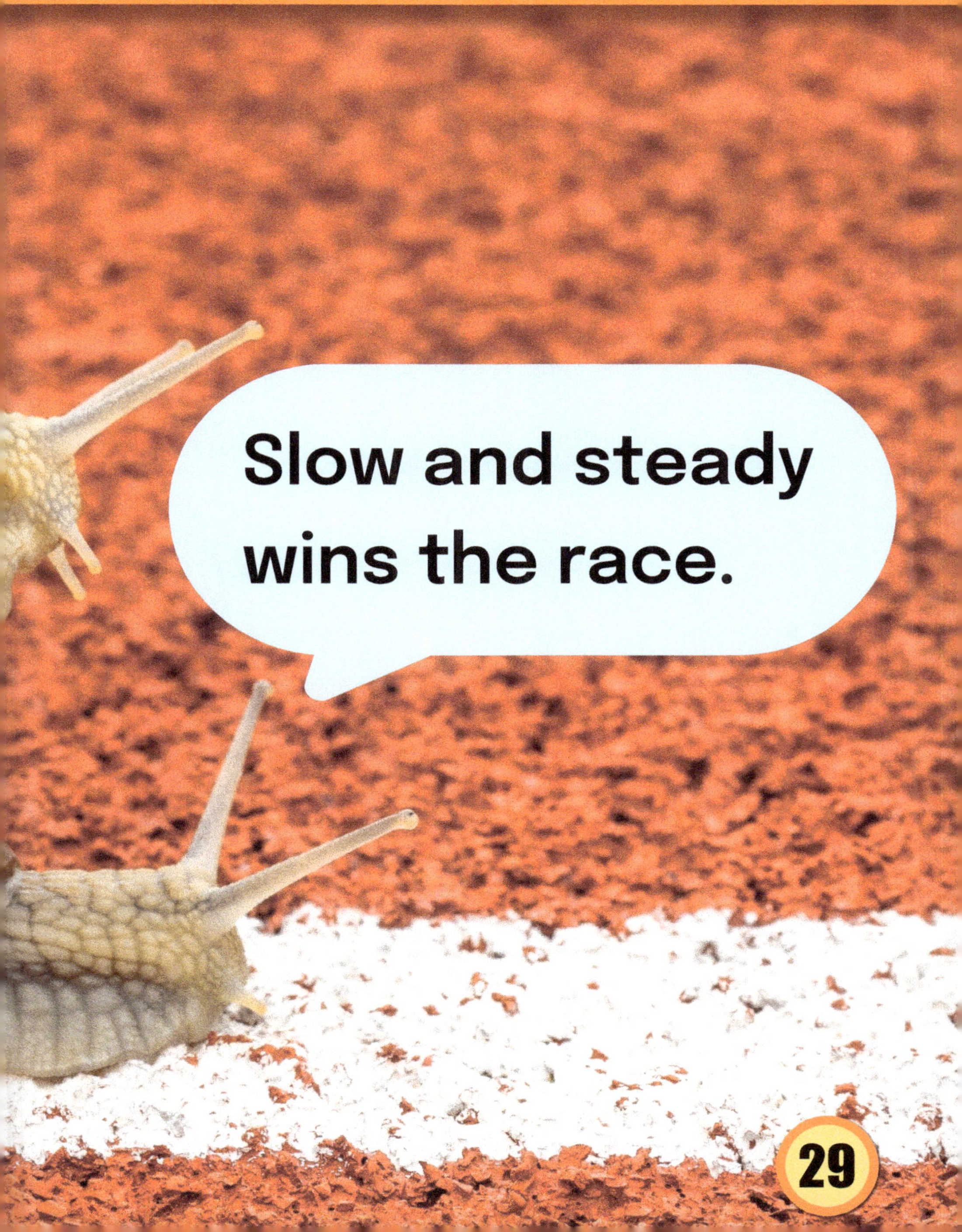

Slow and steady wins the race.

Explore other books in the Backyard Bugs & Creepy Crawlies series!

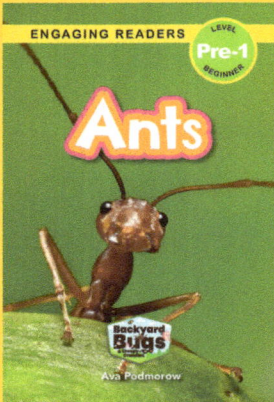

ENGAGING READERS — LEVEL Pre-1 BEGINNER
Ants
Backyard Bugs
Ava Podmorow

ENGAGING READERS — LEVEL Pre-1 BEGINNER
Beetles
Backyard Bugs
Victoria Hazlehurst

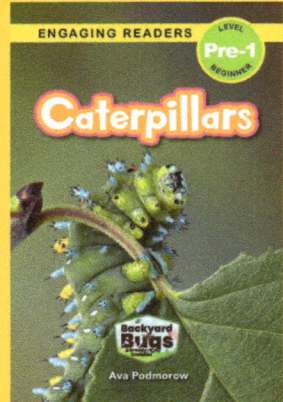

ENGAGING READERS — LEVEL Pre-1 BEGINNER
Caterpillars
Backyard Bugs
Ava Podmorow

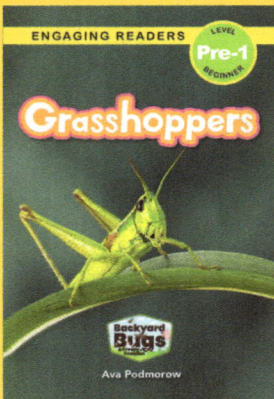

ENGAGING READERS — LEVEL Pre-1 BEGINNER
Grasshoppers
Backyard Bugs
Ava Podmorow

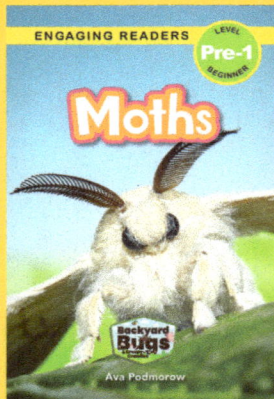

ENGAGING READERS — LEVEL Pre-1 BEGINNER
Moths
Backyard Bugs
Ava Podmorow

ENGAGING READERS — LEVEL Pre-1 BEGINNER
Snails
Backyard Bugs
Ava Podmorow

ENGAGING READERS — LEVEL Pre-1 BEGINNER
Spiders
Backyard Bugs
Ava Podmorow

ENGAGING READERS — LEVEL Pre-1 BEGINNER
Wasps
Backyard Bugs
Sarah Harvey

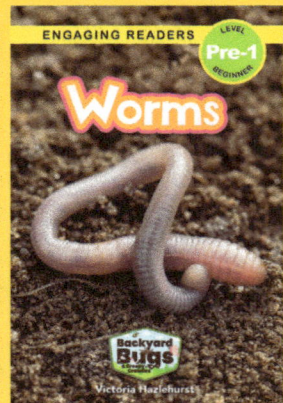

ENGAGING READERS — LEVEL Pre-1 BEGINNER
Worms
Backyard Bugs
Victoria Hazlehurst

Explore books in the Animals In The City series.

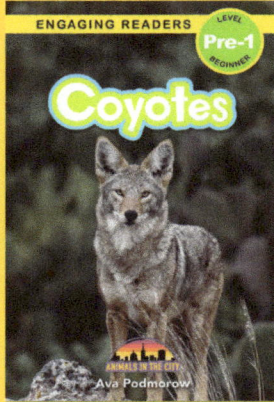

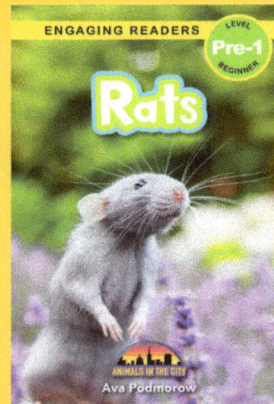

ENGAGING READERS — LEVEL Pre-1 BEGINNER
Cats
Ava Podmorow

ENGAGING READERS — LEVEL Pre-1 BEGINNER
Coyotes
Ava Podmorow

ENGAGING READERS — LEVEL Pre-1 BEGINNER
Deer
Ava Podmorow

ENGAGING READERS — LEVEL Pre-1 BEGINNER
Owls
Ava Podmorow

ENGAGING READERS — LEVEL Pre-1 BEGINNER
Pigeons
Ava Podmorow

ENGAGING READERS — LEVEL Pre-1 BEGINNER
Rabbits
Ava Podmorow

ENGAGING READERS — LEVEL Pre-1 BEGINNER
Raccoons
Sarah Harvey

ENGAGING READERS — LEVEL Pre-1 BEGINNER
Rats
Ava Podmorow

ENGAGING READERS — LEVEL Pre-1 BEGINNER
Skunks
Ava Podmorow

Visit www.engagebooks.com/readers

www.ingramcontent.com/pod-product-compliance
Lightning Source LLC
Chambersburg PA
CBHW051240020426
42331CB00016B/3458